THE P WORD

A Manual for Mammals

Written by David L. Hu, Ph.D.

Illustrated by Ilias Arahovitis

Science, Naturally!
An imprint of Platypus Media, LLC
Washington, D.C.

To my children, Harry and Heidi, who help me grow as a scientist and as a parent.

The P Word: A Manual for Mammals
Hardcover first edition • July 2023 • ISBN: 978-1-938492-78-5
Paperback first edition • August 2024 • ISBN: 978-1-938492-79-2
eBook first edition • July 2023 • ISBN: 978-1-938492-80-8

Written by David L. Hu, Text © 2023
Illustrated by Ilias Arahovitis © 2023

Science Consultant: Diane Kelly, Ph.D., University of Massachusetts Amherst

Also available in Spanish as Empieza con P: Un manual para mamíferos
Spanish paperback first edition • August 2024 • ISBN: 978-1-958629-28-4
Spanish ebook first edition • August 2024 • ISBN: 978-1-958629-61-1

Published in the United States by:
        Science, Naturally! — An imprint of Platypus Media, LLC
        750 First Street NE, Suite 700
        Washington, DC 20002
        202-465-4798 • Fax: 202-558-2132
        Info@ScienceNaturally.com • ScienceNaturally.com

Distributed to the trade by:
        National Book Network (North America)
            301-459-3366 • Toll-free: 800-462-6420
            CustomerCare@NBNbooks.com • NBNbooks.com
        NBN international (worldwide)
            NBNi.Cservs@IngramContent.com • Distribution.NBNi.co.uk

Library of Congress Control Number: 2022947653

10 9 8 7 6 5 4 3 2 1

Schools, libraries, government and non-profit organizations can receive a bulk discount for quantity orders. Contact us at the address above or email us at Info@ScienceNaturally.com.

Printed in China.

Dear Readers,

I wrote this book for my 10-year-old son who, like many other children his age, is eager to learn more about his body. The topics I chose to cover in this book have paralleled many of the conversations I have had with him about the best way to care for himself as he gets older.

There is so much more to the penis than its role in sex. Long before they experience puberty or learn about the "birds and the bees," children are already aware of their body and its functions every time they use the bathroom. It's important not only to learn the purpose and function of the penis, but, additionally, how to best care for this part of the body.

When we look for science, we look for microscopes, telescopes, or inside thick books. However, one of the greatest tools for young scientists to master is the courage to be curious about the world around them. Asking questions about the things we encounter everyday, such as our anatomy, is not only practical, but also provides important scientific training.

To be a good scientist, we can't be afraid of taboo or forbidden topics. We must go directly where our curiosity leads us. Only if we are so fearless, will we have a chance at making the greatest discoveries. There is still so much about the penis to be understood.

So if your child is curious about their penis, encourage them to read this book and keep asking questions. One day they might even uncover one of the answers!

David L. Hu, Ph.D.
Professor of Mechanical
Engineering and Biology
Georgia Institute of Technology

TABLE OF CONTENTS

This book is about the penis, a piece of anatomy found in all mammals. In explaining the care and functioning of this body part, we do not assume that having a penis makes someone a boy. For additional resources about gender, turn to page 52.

WHAT IS A PENIS?

The short answer: it's an **organ**. Just like the heart, lungs, and brain, the **penis** works behind the scenes everyday to keep our bodies safe and healthy.

Unlike most of our other organs, though, we can actually see and touch our penises because it is an external organ (like our eyes and our skin). It has some important jobs.

These jobs include peeing (and for some animals, even **marking** their territory) and **reproduction**.

Because the human penis is not protected inside the body, like most of our other organs, we need to take special care of it to make sure it stays safe and works well.

The Basics of Having a Penis

SO, WHO (OR WHAT!) HAS A PENIS?

We all know that humans have penises—those of us who have one see it every day. When we use the bathroom or change our clothes, it's always right there.

Humans are not the only animals with penises. All **biologically male** mammals have them, but only some insects, birds, and reptiles do.

THAT MEANS...

A TIGER,

A BAT,

A SLOTH,

A KANGAROO,

AND A GORILLA

...ALL HAVE A PENIS!

DO ALL PENISES LOOK THE SAME?

Every penis is unique. Especially among different species, penises come in a wide variety of shapes and sizes.

Humans, apes, and bats have penises that hang outside the body.

Most other mammals' penises are hidden, like in bears, lions, and beavers.

DID YOU KNOW THAT...

Cats have spikes on their penises.

Echidnas have a penis that has four heads.

Vervet monkeys have a dark red penis.

Some whales have penises that can grow up to eight feet long, which is more than two and a half meters.

EVEN AMONG HUMANS, NO PENIS LOOKS THE SAME.

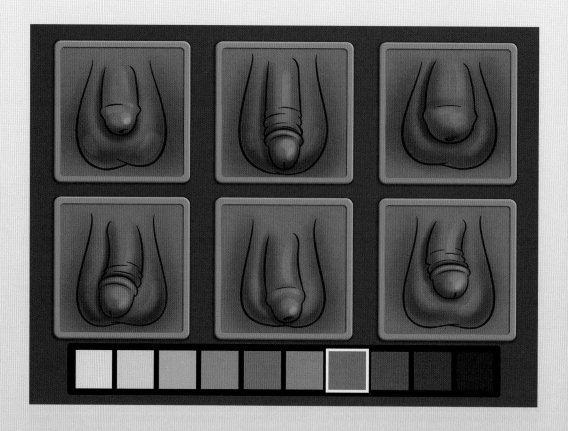

Skin can be a wide variety of colors, and penises can be too!

The color of our penises can be very different from the color of the skin on the rest of our bodies, and the shape can be straight or curved in any direction.

The length, the width, and the size of the **shaft** and **head** can all vary.

Some human penises look different than others at the tip. This is because some kids are circumcised. **Circumcision** is the surgical removal of the **foreskin**, the loose skin that covers the tip of the penis. Each family can decide whether or not to have their child's penis circumcised. Many choose to have it done for religious reasons.

No matter the shape or size, all penises share the same purpose: to keep us healthy.

They do this in many ways. One of the ways our penises help us stay healthy is by getting rid of our **urine**.

WHY DO WE PEE?

The main reason is simple: because we drink water. All mammals, from the smallest shrew to the largest whale, need water to survive. It is essential for keeping our bodies in working order. Without water, we would not be able to digest our food, maintain our body temperature, or keep our cells healthy.

The purpose of peeing, also called **urination** or **micturition**, is to release extra water, salts, and unwanted **toxins** from our bodies.

The main toxin we need to get rid of is called **urea** (it's easy to remember because _ur_ea is in _ur_ine). Urea is made from **ammonia**, a dangerous chemical produced when our bodies break down food and turn it into energy. While ammonia is the chemical that comes from digestion, the liver converts it into urea, a safer form of ammonia.

WAIT A MINUTE—HOW DO WE PEE?

We release urine through our **urinary system** (the organs that create urine and help push it out of our bodies).

Let's start from the top—the **kidneys**.

All mammals are born with two of these bean-shaped organs, located on each side of the backbone, below the ribs and behind the stomach.

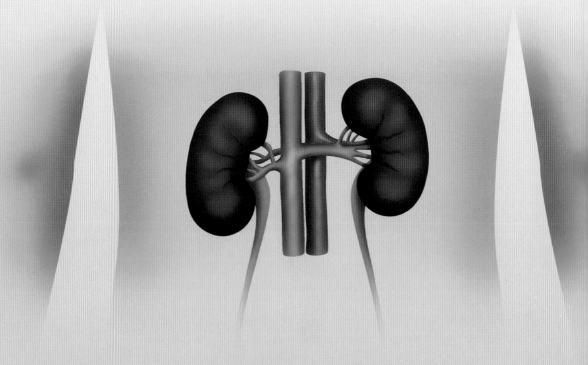

The kidneys' job is to clean our blood. In fact, all the blood in your body passes through the kidneys to be cleaned 40 times every day! During this cleaning, the kidneys collect waste, extra water, and salt from the blood and convert them into urine.

Notice the two tubes coming down from the kidneys? They are the **ureters**.

The ureters are the pathways for the urine to leave the kidneys and enter the **bladder** (a hollow, muscular organ that holds urine until it is emptied) on its way out of the body.

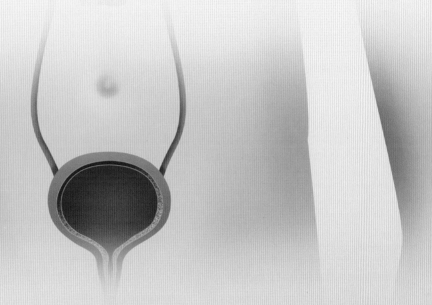

When the bladder is full, the **nervous system** alerts the brain that it is time to empty it. *That's how we know we gotta go!*

There are two ways of releasing urine: actively squeezing the bladder or letting it drain like water in a sink. Our bladder is controlled by a muscle similar to a sink plug called a **sphincter** that, when relaxed, lets the bladder push out the urine. Babies don't have control over this muscle, so when they *gotta go*, they just go (this is where diapers come in handy).

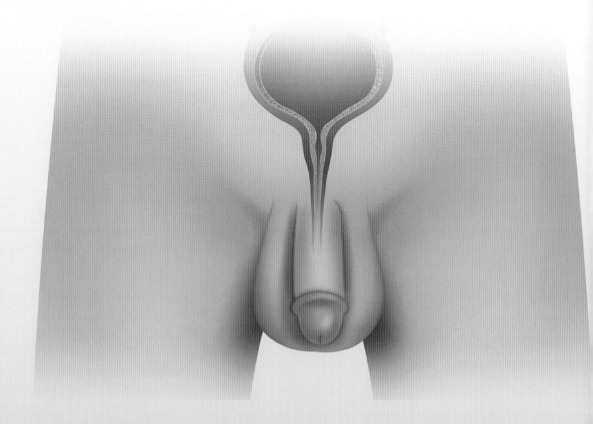

The **urethra** is a tube along the length of the penis. It's the last stop for our urine before it leaves our bodies. The urethra ends with the opening at the tip of the penis where urine is actually released.

A penis lets you pee standing up. This is probably its best design feature—especially if you are out in the woods! The urethra generally points downward and away from our bodies. Just like water flows down a water slide, urine follows the path of the urethra inside the penis and arcs through the air until it lands.

The color of our pee is determined by the amount of water we drink, the foods we eat, and the vitamins that are in those foods. Typically, pee appears as several shades of yellow, depending on how **hydrated** we are. The darker our pee, the less water we have in our bodies. That means dark yellow pee is a clue that you need to drink more water.

And this is universal! All mammals pee in some shade of yellow—not just humans.

Pee color can also be affected by eating certain foods, like beets, blackberries, rhubarb, and fava beans.

For some people, eating asparagus changes the smell of their pee (and not in a good way!).

The 21 Second Rule

HOW LONG DO WE PEE?

Research (ahem, the author's!) has found that all mammals over 3 kilograms, or about 7 pounds, urinate for 21 seconds at a time, on average. *On average* means the time may be longer or shorter, but 21 seconds is typical.

HUMAN	**LION**	**ZEBRA**
23 seconds	36 seconds	8 seconds
500 mL / .13 gal	2125 mL / .56 gal	4250 mL / 1.12 gal

Mammals on the larger side drink more than smaller mammals and have larger bladders, so they have more urine they need to release. However, a longer urethra allows them to release the urine at a faster speed. So, for most mammals large or small (so long as they're over 3 kilograms), the time spent peeing doesn't actually change much.

INDIAN RHINOCEROS
20 seconds
9000 mL / 2.38 gal

ELEPHANT
22 seconds
18000 mL / 4.76 gal

PEEING IN FLIGHT

No matter where we are or what we're doing, we need to pee about six to eight times everyday. Even if we try to hold our bladders for as long as possible, our bodies will release urine when they need to.

So what happens when we aren't near a bathroom— *or even on our planet?*

Fighter pilots may need to pee while they're in the cockpit. This is when a Piddle Pack, a sealable plastic bag with absorbent beads, comes in handy.

There's even a mammal that pees in flight—bats. While they are out of their roosts, bats will pee in the air. When they are in their roosts, bats flip rightside up and pee hanging by their thumbs. *One lesson we've learned here: always keep our heads covered around bats!*

And how do astronauts pee? Well, when they are out in space, they actually have to wear special adult diapers under their space suits (they aren't just for babies!).

Diapers work very well, but no adult likes to wear them. Scientists are constantly working on new devices to manage pee. The NASA Space Poop Challenge is one way scientists work to create a spacesuit that would empty the pee and poop automatically to keep the astronaut clean.

PEEING UNDER THE SEA

How do scuba divers use the bathroom?

Mostly, they just pee in their wetsuits. This keeps divers from needing to rush back to shore and cut their dive short! Then, they'll wash their suits after they get out of the water.

So do whales and other marine mammals pee?

Yes. It probably comes as no surprise that whales produce more pee than any other animal, since they are the largest.

Is all that pee bad for the ocean?

It isn't! While too much pee from animals that live on land (such as cows and pigs) can hurt the **ocean ecosystem**, the pee of whales, fish, seals, and other marine animals is actually healthy for it.

Whales pee near the surface of the water, and it provides TONS of nutrients for fish—the whales' urine actually helps feed microscopic plants called **phytoplankton**, which then feed many fish. It also helps keep coral reefs alive and healthy.

PEEING IN THE WILD

Have you ever noticed a Spray Zone sign at the zoo?

This sign is there to let humans know that animals—such as lions and tigers—mark their territory by peeing.

If you get too close, they might accidentally mark you!

Humans also like to mark their territory. We usually do this by finding a place to call home. It may be separated from other areas by a wall, fence, or yard.

Most people are happy to just enjoy their space, but others want to make sure everyone knows that they should stay away. They may post *"No Trespassing"* or *"Keep Off My Property"* signs.

Mammals are the same way. Most just go about living their lives in their **habitat**, but some want to make it very clear that no outsiders should step foot (or paw or hoof) into their "home." Instead of putting up a sign, they use their penises to mark their home with urine as a way of communicating with nearby animals.

BUT HUMANS DON'T USE OUR PENISES TO MARK TERRITORY?

That's true! While humans have found lots of ways to mark our homes without urine, many mammals still use their penises to spray an area and claim it as their own.

Humans don't have a highly sensitive olfactory (*sense of smell*) system. What simply smells like pee to us can actually tell other mammals a lot. Just by sniffing a mammal's spray, animals can tell the species, and even the health and strength, of the animal that left its mark.

That's why our dogs spend so much time sniffing other dogs' rear ends and neighbors' mailboxes, and making sure to pee just a little bit everywhere they can.

UNIQUE MAMMAL MARKINGS

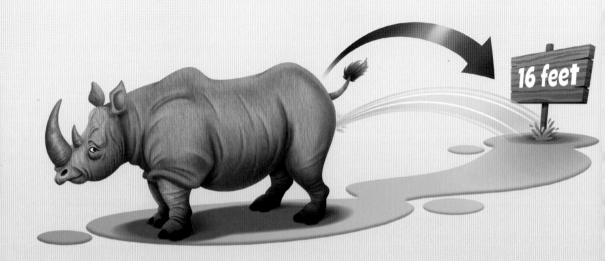

Tigers and rhinoceroses use their penises to spray their urine backward to cover as much distance as possible.

Some Indian rhinoceroses have been able to spray their urine up to 16 feet (which is almost five meters)!

Cat owners are all too familiar with smelly litter boxes, but what's the reason for the stench?

A chemical called *felinine* in cat pee that grows in smelliness over time. In the wild, felinine helps a cat mark their territory by keeping the scent around longer, but for indoor cats, it sure can stink up the house.

Bearcats, a member of the civet family, are known for having urine that smells like buttered popcorn. The movie theater smell comes from a chemical called *2AP*. As they pee, their urine—and the chemical—gets on their tails and paws. Trailing this scent around helps nearby bearcats know that another one is around.

So now we know that peeing can be a form of communication. Whether it's our bladder telling us *it's time to go* or a mammal's urine telling other mammals *stay out*, pee can say a lot!

Just like pee, our penises tell us what's going on in our bodies. And sometimes our penises even change shape or size to indicate a change in our brains... but how does that work?

WHAT DOES IT MEAN WHEN OUR PENISES GET HARD OR STIFF?

This is called an **erection,** and having one is totally normal. Basically, an erection is the way a penis exercises itself. Our bodies are constantly working to keep us healthy, but a lot of that work happens behind the scenes. Because our penises are outside of our bodies, erections are more obvious to us than our hearts pumping our blood or our muscles contracting and relaxing.

Erections are a natural reaction our bodies have to our environment. They can be the result of a touch or a thought, or they can even happen for no particular reason and with no advance warning.

SO, HOW DOES AN ERECTION HAPPEN?

Think of how blood rushes to your head when you do a handstand. Getting an erection is a similar experience, except it is a rush of blood to the penis.

Blood flows through what is called the **corpus cavernosum**, a maze of spongy tissue and blood vessels. As the penis fills with blood, it begins to harden and rise.

All adults know what erections are and understand that they are a natural part of life. Don't feel embarrassed to bring up your questions with a parent, doctor, or adult you trust.

No one should look at or touch your body or penis without your **consent.** For example, you wouldn't give someone a hug unless they gave you their permission. If you are uncomfortable with anyone asking to see or touch your penis or for you to see or touch theirs, you do not have to give consent. Tell them NO! If you are worried that someone isn't listening to you when you do not give consent, or isn't asking for your consent at all, talk to a trusted adult.

ERECTIONS IN THE WILD

Though we are close relatives with other mammal species, erections in the wild can look very different from what humans are used to.

For some mammals, an erection isn't only the result of increased blood flow. Many mammals have a bone called a **baculum** inside the penis that helps make it stiff, including this gray wolf (although it's hard to see under all that fur).

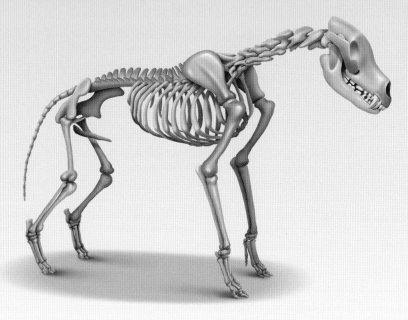

WHY DOES AN ERECTION HAPPEN?

Our bodies undergo a lot of changes as we grow into healthy adults.

For most of childhood, erections come and go, often without us even noticing.

But everything changes around the age of 10...

WHAT HAPPENS THEN?

Puberty! We've all heard the word and know that it means our bodies are going to change in important ways: puberty is the transition of our bodies from childhood to adulthood.

These changes happen on a different timeline for everyone. It may be as early as nine or as late as 14, but no matter when it happens, puberty is a natural part of growing up.

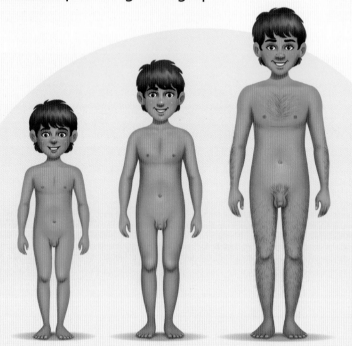

Puberty usually begins because our bodies start producing a **hormone** called **testosterone**. Once this happens, we start to grow taller, our voices may get deeper, and we may notice hair under our arms, on our faces, and around our **pubic area** (learn more about this area and the body parts included in it on page 54).

Because puberty is the biggest period of growth, the penis, **scrotum**, and **testicles** will grow. During and after puberty, the size, length, or width of the penis and testicles may change. Small or large, thick or thin, different sizes, lengths, and widths are all common and healthy.

WHAT DOES THIS HAVE TO DO WITH ERECTIONS?

When we hit puberty, our erections will lead to what's called **ejaculation**, or the release of **semen**.

Even though we don't start to produce sperm and semen until puberty, it is important to understand how our bodies work at all ages so we are better prepared for the changes to come.

Semen is one of the two liquids that comes from our penises (the other is urine). It is a complex mixture that contains millions of special cells called **sperm** that are used in reproduction.

Like a factory, the testicles are the first step to create and "package" sperm to be sent out.

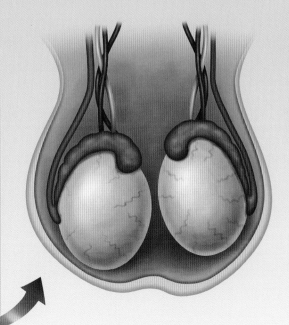

Testicles are inside a pouch of skin called the scrotum, which can act like our own thermometer! If it's cold outside, the scrotum pulls the testicles closer to the body. If it's warm outside, the testicles hang away from the body.

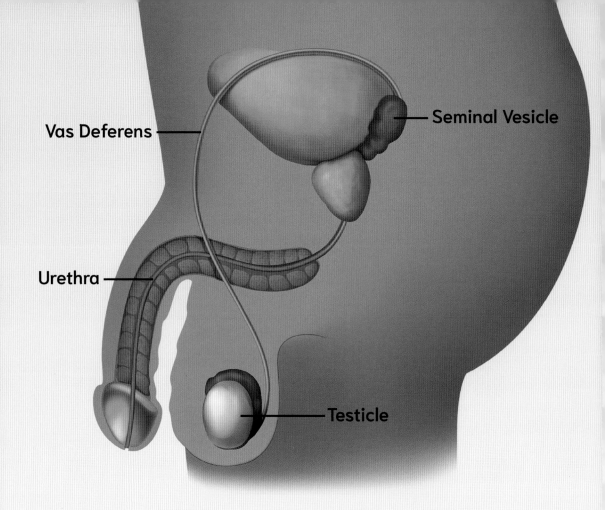

Vas Deferens —— · Seminal Vesicle

Urethra —

Testicle

When the sperm is ready to be delivered, it travels from the testicles through the **vas deferens**. This muscular tube goes over and around the bladder and connects to the urethra.

The vas deferens is like a train track for sperm to follow on its way to the **seminal vesicle.** This is where semen and sperm combine. Semen's primary role is to keep the sperm cells healthy as they leave the body through ejaculation.

We might first experience ejaculation as the result of a **wet dream.** We'll wake up with a wet, sticky spot on our pajamas or sheets, but we haven't peed in bed. If this happens, it just means that we had an erection and ejaculated while we were asleep.

HOW DOES SEMEN SPEED STACK UP?

Farts	Semen	Cough	Sneeze
11 kph / 9 mph	45 kph / 28 mph	100 kph / 62 mph	160 kph / 100 mph

HOW ABOUT THE MAMMAL WORLD?

As we know, humans have testicles that hang outside their bodies, but for some mammals, the testicles aren't visible. While some are hidden by fur and tucked away between their legs (like the gray wolf), others (like elephants) have testicles that are actually inside their bodies.

Similar to humans, most mammals have testicles outside of their bodies, however their scrotums often come in different shapes and sizes. The vervet monkey has a bright blue scrotum—the most colorful of all mammals.

WHY DO OUR BODIES CREATE SPERM AND RELEASE SEMEN?

To reproduce!

Reproduction is what makes human life possible and is necessary for the survival of all living things. For mammals, a key piece of making offspring lies within semen.

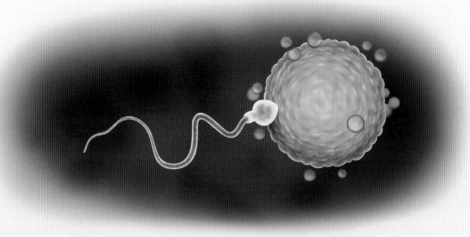

To produce offspring, a sperm cell needs to connect with an egg. Not every ejaculation will lead to reproduction because sperm alone cannot produce offspring.

When joined with an egg, the combination carries all the instructions and ingredients to start growing a mammal's offspring.

Even though the reproductive system is essential to keeping a species alive, unlike other body systems, it's not essential to keeping an individual alive.

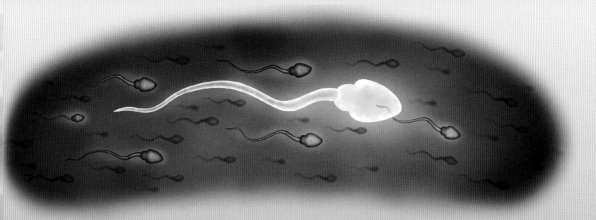

Sperm are teeny, tiny swimming cells. Even though only a small amount of semen comes out with each ejaculation, it can contain up to 900 million sperm cells. The body continuously makes new sperm well into old age.

REPRODUCTION IN THE MAMMAL WORLD

European rabbits can have up to 130 babies in their lifetime (imagine having that many siblings!).

Orangutans reproduce the least of all non-human mammals, having only one baby every 6–8 years.

HOW CAN WE KEEP THE PENIS IN TIP-TOP SHAPE?

We wash and keep clean not only because we get dirt on ourselves throughout the day, but also to get rid of germs like **bacteria** and **viruses.**

Germs can make us sick and affect us year-round. Soap, water, and regular bathing keeps germs away and helps our bodies stay healthy. Each time you visit the bathroom, even if you don't poop, it's important to wash your hands with soap.

One way bacteria can affect the penis is through a **urinary tract infection**. These infections, also known as UTIs, are caused by bacteria entering the bladder, urethra, or in some serious cases, the kidneys. Experiencing pain while peeing could be a symptom of a UTI.

As we get older, there are a number of diseases that one person can give to another. Just as one person can give another a cold, penis infections can be passed between those who have close contact with someone else's pubic area.

Stay Healthy, Stay Clean!

When peeing:

- Be courteous. Pee into urinals rather than next to them.
- When using the toilet, lift the seat to pee and aim into the toilet.
- If you miss, make sure to clean it up—the next user will appreciate it!

When taking a shower:

- Wash your penis with just a little bit of gentle soap, and make sure to rinse it all off.
- If your penis still has a foreskin, wash underneath it at least a couple times a week.

Notice a whitish material around the foreskin? That's called **smegma**, and it means it's time to wash!

ALL MAMMALS KEEP THEIR PENISES CLEAN!

As we know, humans, apes, and bats, and even cats and dogs, have penises that are exposed and unprotected, so keeping them clean is especially important.

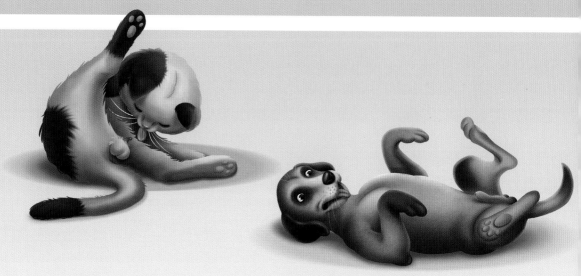

Cats and dogs often lick their penises after peeing to keep them clean and healthy.

Budongo chimpanzees use leaves as napkins to clean their penises.

KEEPING THE PENIS SAFE IN THE WILD AND ON THE FIELD!

Mammals walk on four feet, fly in the air, or swim in the sea, and most are able to retract their penises when they are not in use to keep them safe.

Humans do not have this **adaptation** so we rely on clothing and other protective gear to guard our exposed private parts.

Many contact sports, such as football, baseball, hockey, and fencing, require athletes to wear special equipment to protect their pubic area. The **jockstrap** is made up of an elastic band and a hard plastic cup and keeps the penis from getting injured if it gets hit.

HAVE WE LEARNED EVERYTHING?
WHAT ELSE COULD THERE BE TO LEARN?

This book is just an introduction to one of the many organs that keep us alive and healthy.

The penis gets rid of waste, marks territories, creates new life, and communicates to you about your health.

Knowing its important role in keeping us healthy is essential to having pride and respect for this organ.

Throughout our lives, the penis grows and changes. You have learned some new vocabulary and increased your understanding of the inner workings of the body, but there is always more to learn. The best thing we can do is to keep learning and continuing to be curious about our ever-changing bodies.

GLOSSARY

Adaptation – A biological process where living things change in order to survive in their habitat, usually over a long period of time.

Ammonia – A chemical produced when the body breaks down food and turns it into energy; it has no color, but it does have a strong odor.

Bacteria – Simple, microscopic living things; most have important roles in Earth's ecology, but some can make a person sick.

Baculum – A bone found in the penis of many mammals.

Biologically male – A term used to describe people and animals who were born with XY chromosomes and male reproductive organs.

Bladder – A hollow, muscular organ in the pelvis that holds urine until it is emptied.

Circumcision – The removal of the foreskin of the penis, typically soon after the baby's birth.

Consent – To agree or give permission to a person for something to occur.

Corpus cavernosum – The tissue along the shaft of the penis that contains maze-like blood vessels that fill with blood to create an erection.

Ejaculation – The release of semen.

Erection – The hardening of the penis as it fills with blood, usually as a response to a stimulus.

Foreskin – A layer of skin covering the head of the penis. The foreskin is present at birth, but some parents have it removed. See **Circumcision**.

Habitat – The natural environment where an animal, plant, or other organism lives.

Head of the penis – Also known as the *glans*; the rounded tip that is a little wider than the rest of the penis.

Hormones – Special chemicals that control and regulate the activity of specific cells or organs in the body to keep it working properly.

Hydrated – Having enough water inside the body for its organs to work properly.

Jockstrap – Special underwear to protect the penis and pubic area while playing sports.

Kidneys – The two bean-shaped organs, located on each side of the spine below the rib cage, that clean the blood by collecting waste and extra water; this is then converted into urine.

Marking – Also known as spraying; a behavior used by animals to notify other animals that they have claimed an area or object.

Micturition – Also called urination; the process of releasing urine from the bladder.

Nervous system – Highly complex system that tells the body what to do and how to move by sending signals between different body parts.

Ocean ecosystem – The web of life that connects all things that live in the ocean; the ocean ecosystem is the largest ecosystem in the world.

Organ – A self-contained group of cells and tissues inside of a body that perform a specific vital function.

Penis – An organ located in the groin area, made up of the head, foreskin, and shaft.

Phytoplankton – Tiny microscopic plants that are food for many different parts of the ocean ecosystem.

Puberty – The period of life, usually between ages nine to 14, when a child starts to experience changes in their body, including physical changes and hormonal changes, that mark the transition to adulthood.

Pubic area – Also known as the groin; the area of the hip between the stomach and thigh; in biological males, it includes the penis and testicles.

Reproduction – A biological process that creates new life; in humans and other mammals, this occurs when a sperm cell connects with an egg.

Scrotum – The skin that hangs below and behind the penis and holds the testicles.

Semen – A liquid that comes from the penis that contains sperm and the nutrients to keep sperm healthy.

Seminal vesicle – The organ along the bottom of the bladder; this is where sperm is combined with nutrients to make semen.

Shaft – The main part of the penis that extends from the lower belly to the tip of the head and contains the urethra and corpus cavernosm.

Smegma – A thick, white substance composed of shed skin cells, skin oils, and moisture that collects under the foreskin.

Sperm – Tiny swimming cells contained in semen; reproduction begins when a sperm cell connects with an egg.

Sphincter – A muscle that can open and close certain parts of the body, such as the bladder.

Testicles – Also known as testes or gonads; they produce sperm and testosterone.

Testosterone – A hormone produced mainly in the testes that is crucial to puberty and the body's development; tells the body to begin creating sperm and semen.

Toxins – Highly concentrated waste products that are dangerous if they build up and remain in the body.

Urea – A waste product found in urine that is created when the liver breaks down ammonia.

Ureters – The tubes that carry urine from the kidneys to the bladder.

Urethra – The tube that runs from the bladder along the shaft of the penis and carries urine and semen out of the body.

Urinary system – The group of organs that work together to produce urine and help push it out of the body.

Urinary tract infection (UTI) – A painful infection caused by bacteria in any part of the urinary system: kidneys, bladder, ureters, or urethra.

Urination – Also called micturition; the process of releasing urine from the bladder.

Urine – A watery liquid created by kidneys that is full of excess water, salt, and unwanted toxins. It is stored in and eventually released by the bladder.

Vas deferens – A long tube that transports sperm to the urethra to prepare for ejaculation.

Viruses – Microscopic organisms that can only reproduce inside living cells; some types of viruses can cause disease.

Wet dream – Ejaculating, or releasing semen, while asleep.

ADDITIONAL RESOURCES

We probably haven't answered all your questions, but hopefully we've started a conversation. Here are some resources to learn even more:

- Amaze.org

- *Growing Up Great!: The Ultimate Puberty Book for Boys* by Scott Todnem

- TED Talk: What we didn't know about penis anatomy

- PlanetPuberty.org.au

- YouTube: Khan Academy – Anatomy of the Male Reproductive System

- KidsHealth.org

For information about gender, explore these resources:

- GenderSpectrum.org

- *Ana on the Edge* by A.J. Sass

- *I Am Jazz* by Jazz Jennings

- *Jack (Not Jackie)* by Erica Silverman

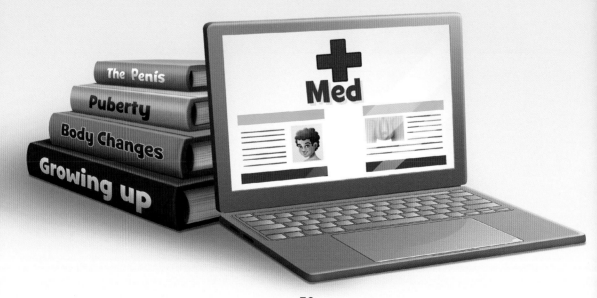

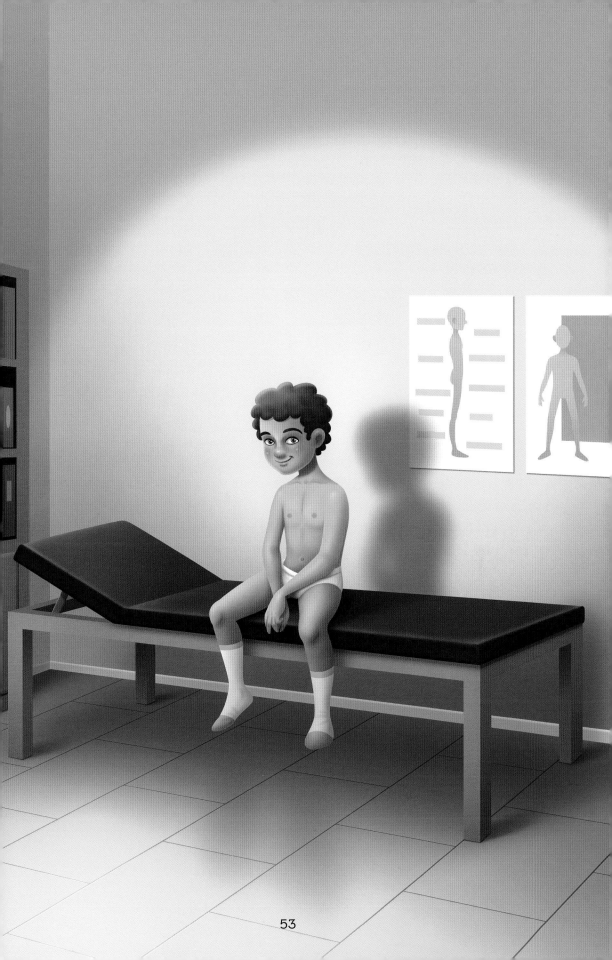

THE ANATOMY OF THE PENIS

1 **Pubic Area or Groin**
The area of the hip between the stomach and thigh, located where the belly ends and the legs begin. This area, like the underarms, has no hair in children, but then grows hair during puberty.

2 **Penis**
The penis has three parts: the head, foreskin, and shaft. It has three main jobs: to carry urine out of the body, to mark territory, and to deliver sperm for reproduction.

3 **Head**
The head of the penis is the rounded tip, and it's also called the *glans.* It is a little wider than the rest of the penis. The tip of the head is where urine is released.

4 **Foreskin**
At birth, the penis has a hood of skin, called the foreskin, which covers the head of the penis. Some parents choose to have the foreskin removed soon after birth. This is called circumcision. It is a common practice in some places and almost unknown in others.

5 **Shaft**
The main part of the penis is called the shaft. It extends from the lower belly to the base of the head. The urethra, the tube that carries urine from the bladder out of the body when you pee, runs along the length of the shaft.

6 **Scrotum**
The scrotum is the skin that hangs below and behind the penis. It holds the testicles and keeps them at the right temperature.

7 **Testicles**
The testicles are inside of the scrotum. These are two round organs that are responsible for producing sperm and testosterone.

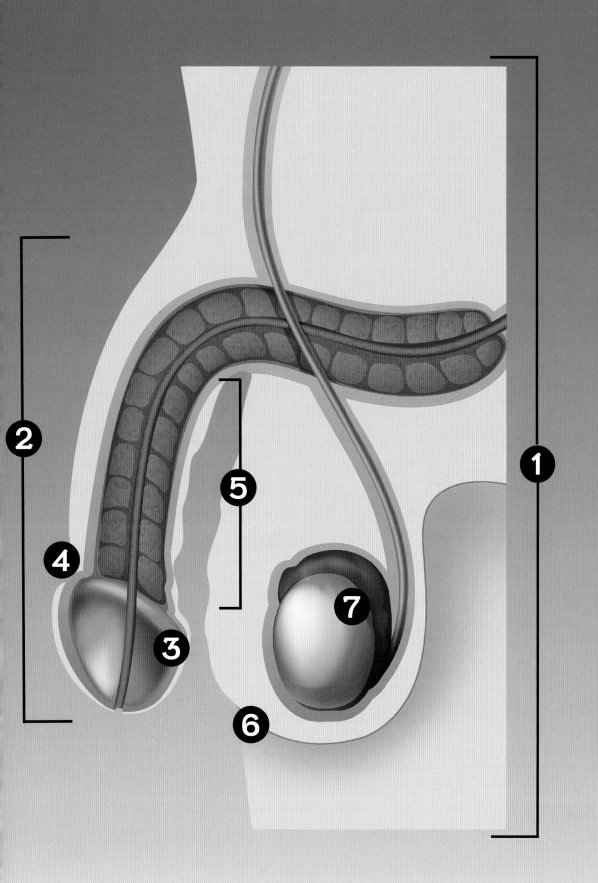

DR. DAVID L. HU is a mechanical engineer and biologist who studies the interactions of animals with water. He has discovered how dogs shake dry, how insects walk on water, and how eyelashes protect the eyes from drying. During his career, he's won the Ig Nobel Prize in Physics, the National Science Foundation CAREER Award, and the Pineapple Science Prize.

Dr. Hu's research has been featured in *The Economist*, *The New York Times*, *Saturday Night Live*, *Science Friday*, and *Highlights for Children*. He is the author of the young adult nonfiction book *How to Walk on Water and Climb Up Walls*. A professor at Georgia Institute of Technology, Dr. Hu lives with his wife and two children in Atlanta, Georgia. He can be reached at David.Hu@ScienceNaturally.com.

ILIAS ARAHOVITIS was born in South Africa and was raised in Athens, Greece. In his early years, Ilias's canvas was the floor and walls, but after the age of five, he started using actual canvas to create his first oil paintings. Ilias graduated from AKTO Art & Design College in Athens, and now specializes in children's books, having illustrated numerous books in the last 25 years.

"Some body parts confuse people. Some amuse people. Professor David L. Hu, a great scientist, makes this book about a world famous body part both fun and informative. *The P Word* is sure to un-confuse *and* amuse you!"

  —Marc Abrahams, Founder, The Ig Nobel Prizes
   Editor and Co-founder, Annals of Improbable Research, Cambridge, MA

"As a psychiatrist and emergency room physician, I thought I knew the human body well... that was until I read David L. Hu's original and highly accessible book. Hu has managed the near-impossible: creating a family-friendly picture book that engages and informs audiences of all ages. *The P Word* is the definitive introduction to the penis that is both scientifically precise and delightfully entertaining!"

  —Jacob M. Appel, M.D., Associate Professor of Psychiatry,
   Icahn School of Medicine, New York, NY

"*The P Word* is a delightful book that presents scientific information about the penis in age-appropriate, accessible, and inclusive language. The book's light-hearted and matter-of-fact tone is sure to help break taboos in talking about bodies and will help young people learn to take care of themselves as they grow and develop."

  —Nicole Cushman, M.P.H., Sexual Health Educator, New York, NY

"Many parents sidestep and dodge 'the p word' conversation with their growing children. However, as kids explore their anatomy and try to understand the changes that are beginning to occur, they need a reliable guide to clarify the mysteries of the body. Professor David L. Hu is a world-renowned biomechanist who is not afraid to examine what some consider too icky to talk about. This candid book answers any questions kids may have about their penis—without them even having to ask!"

  —Frank E. Fish, Ph.D., Recipient, 2022 Ig Nobel Prize in Physics,
   Professor of Biology, West Chester University, PA

"This immensely informative book delves into the topic of the penis—what it is, how it works, and how to keep it healthy. Though a science book at heart, the author presents the material with an unusually sensitive comfort and lightness. Curiosity-piquing headings, illustrations, and insights, many of which revolve around non-human mammals, make for the sort of page-turner rarely encountered in children's nonfiction."

  —Dan Levy, Program Director, Tillywig Toy and Media Awards

"Brilliant! My 9-year-old boy was fascinated and I even learned a thing or two as well. The colorful and tasteful illustrations are excellent. The presentation of the material is age-appropriate and the topics covered (e.g. anatomy, peeing in outer space, marking your territory, etc.) are cleverly organized."

  —Academics' Choice Awards Reviewer

WHAT THE EXPERTS ARE SAYING

"What a kid-friendly, amusing, and educational read—for both kids and adults! *The P Word* does a great job covering the science of anatomy and puberty in an informative, friendly, and light-hearted manner. Parents will appreciate that it addresses topics they might feel nervous or hesitant about discussing. I wish this book had been available earlier in my teaching career."

— Alexandra Roosenburg, M.T., M.Ed., Founder and Director
Capitol Learning Academy, Washington, D.C.

"If human anatomy is a taboo topic in your household, this terrific little book will change your life for the better. Delightfully written and perfectly illustrated, it explains everything you always wanted to know about the penis but were afraid to ask. Scientifically sound, it also provides lots of good information about other mammals. *The P Word* should be required reading for all 10-year-olds and many adults!"

— Don E. Wilson, Ph.D., Curator Emeritus of Mammals,
National Museum of Natural History, Washington D.C.

"As a pediatrician, I know the importance of sharing accurate and appropriate resources with my patients and their families. Kids will enjoy learning about the 'p word' at a level they can understand. I highly recommend this refreshingly honest and engaging book!"

— Jennifer A.F. Tender, M.D., Pediatrician, Washington, D.C.

"A unique and fascinating book! Parents will learn along with their children as they read this wonderfully informative book together. The fun facts about varied mammals'—and particularly humans'—urinary and reproductive organs are engaging and extremely well presented."

— A. Heather He. Halperin, M.S.W., L.C.S.W., Retired Faculty
USC Suzanne Dworak-Peck School of Social Work, Los Angeles, CA

"*The P Word* is a delightful book. It will go far in helping kids understand how their bodies work. Sensitively written, funny, and informative, this book will inspire kids—before, during, and after puberty—to be comfortable in their own skin!"

— John Santelli, M.D., M.P.H., Population and Family Health and Pediatrics
Mailman School of Public Health, Columbia University

"As a pediatric urologist, I see many families whose children are having issues with their urinary tract system or reproductive organs. Educating them about how their bodies work and how to keep them healthy is always the first step, especially when going number one is the number one priority! David L. Hu does a marvelous job of presenting sensitive information with accuracy and a sense of humor."

— David I. Chu, M.D., M.S.C.E., Pediatric Urology, Chicago, IL